—— main road
— secondary road

COMINO

M E D I T E R R A N E A N S E A

Mielieha Bay

Is-Sellum

Ta l-Blata

ellieha   Xemxija

St. Paul's Bay

Bugibba

M A L T A

Mgarr   Zebbiegh

Burmarrad

Gharghur

St. Julian's

Naxxar   San Gwann   Gzira   Sliema

Mosta

Marsamxett harbour

Birkirkara   **VALLETTA**

Mdina   Hamrun   *The Grand harbour*   Vittoriosa

Senglea   Cospicua

Rabat   Hal-Qormi   Zabbar

Haz-Zebbug

Marsaskala

Luqa   Il-Kappana

Dingli   Zejtun

Siggiewi   Hal-Ghaxaq

Mqabba   Gudja   Marsaxlokk

Hal-Kirkop

Orendi   Hal-Safi

Zurrieq   Birzebbuga

0   5 km

0   5 miles

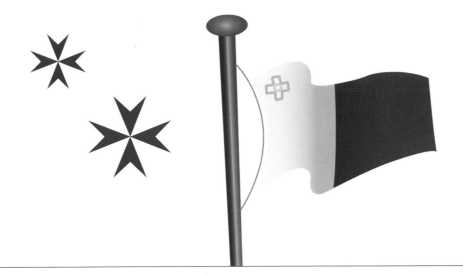

New EU Countries and Citizens

Malta

Jan Willem Bultje

A Cherrytree Book

This edition published in 2006 by Evans Brothers Limited
2A Portman Mansions
Chiltern Street
London W1U 6NR, UK

Published by arrangement with KIT Publishers, The Netherlands

British Library Cataloguing-in-Publication Data
Bultje, Jan Willem
Malta. - (New EU countries and citizens)
1. Malta - Juvenile literature
I. Title
945.8'5
ISBN 1842343262
9781842343265

Text: Jan Willem Bultje
Photographs: Jan Willem Bultje
Translation: Linda Cook
UK editing: Sonya Newland
Design and Layout: Grafisch Ontwerpbureau Agaatsz BNO, Meppel, The Netherlands
Cover: Big Blu Ltd
Cartography: Armand Haye, Amsterdam, The Netherlands
Production: J & P Far East Productions, Soest, The Netherlands

Picture Credits

Photographs: Jan Willem Bultje
p.34 (l,b): Epa Photo; Lino Arrigo Azzopardi; p.22 (b), 23 (b), 24, 27 (t), 33 (b), 40, 42, Malta
Tourist Authority; p. 24 © Bob Krist/CORBIS; p. 39(t) © Michael Gore; Frank Lane Picture
Agency/CORBIS

Contents

Introduction

Malta's strategic location in the Mediterranean, easily accessible from the coasts of Sicily and north-east Africa, has resulted in it being invaded and occupied by several different peoples in its long history. However, Malta has survived all the change and conflict, and this group of tiny islands is now an independent republic.

Situated right in the middle of the Mediterranean Sea, Malta lies just 100 km south of the island of Sicily and 290 km to the east of Tunisia in North Africa. People have built communities on Malta since the Stone Age and the influence of the many peoples who have settled there is still evident all over the island – from the ancient stone temples of the megalithic tribes to the British traditions left over from when Malta was a Crown Colony. Malta has a high population density, made up of ethnically diverse groups, including Arabs, British, Italian, Spanish and Sicilian.

Three islands make up what we call Malta. Malta itself is the largest island; Gozo is about one third of the size of Malta and is situated to the north. In between Malta and Gozo lies the small island of Comino, which is barely inhabited.

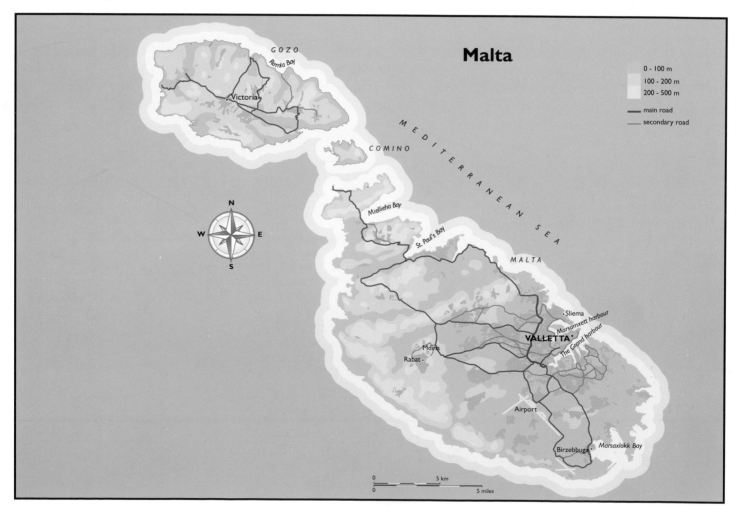

The capital of Malta was once the combined cities of Rabat and Mdina, known as Melita, but the Knights of St John moved the capital to Valletta in the sixteenth century and built a fortified city there to protect themselves against attacks by the Muslim Turks. The knights play an important role in the history of Malta – they lived on the island for several centuries, during a time of great wealth and prosperity. The Maltese commemorate the knights in exhibitions and pageants.

Malta became a Crown Colony – under the rule of the British – in 1814. The British influence can still be felt in many places on the island, and is reflected in ways of life such as the Maltese system of education. Most people on Malta speak English, although their own language – Maltese – shows the influence of other peoples who have lived there, notably the Arabs.

▲ *The Dingli Cliffs were named after the English knight Thomas Dingli, and are the highest point on Malta, at 253 metres.*

Because the Maltese islands are so small, they cannot rely on large amounts of trade and export to maintain their economy. Tourism is now one of the most important of the islands' industries and every year around one million people travel to Malta to enjoy the warm weather, the magnificent scenery and the hundreds of historical sites. Malta's accession to the European Union on 1 May 2004 was an important event in the country's history. Improved relationships with other EU countries should result in a longer-term improvement in the economy, as well as in other important areas such as transport, employment and environmental issues.

◄ *A view of Rabat and Mdina, the cities that were once the capital of the island of Malta. In the centre is the dome of St Paul's Church.*

History

There have been people living on Malta for more than 7,000 years. The first Maltese were farmers who probably came from Sicily, an island 100 km north of Malta, around 5200 BC. They lived in caves, kept cattle and made pottery. Fragments of pottery have been found in some of the caves on the island.

▼ *The Mnajdra temple complex can be found on the south coast of Malta and dates from around 3500 BC. There are three temples here, where priests and priestesses would have conducted ancient religious ceremonies.*

During the Stone Age, around 3600 BC, a tribe of people from the megalithic culture arrived on Malta. They built temples using enormous stones – some of them weighing as much as 50,000 kilos – in honour of their goddess of fertility. The temples are among the oldest surviving stone structures in the world – more than a millennium older than the Egyptian pyramids.

Over the course of time, the temple builders and the islands' original inhabitants intermingled, and after about 1,000 years, the temple culture was lost. The next newcomers to the island, around 1000 BC, were the Phoenicians – sea merchants who lived on the coast of what is now Lebanon. They called the island 'Malat', which means 'safe harbour', and set up trading posts there.

▶ *Hagar Qim was built around 2800* BC. *It is a circular complex made up of four temples with two opposite entrances.*

Roman rule

The Romans took possession of Malta in 218 BC. They renamed it 'Melita', which means 'honey island', and built villas and public baths there. The capital city of the same name was built in the middle of the island. During the period of Roman rule there was a shipwreck that proved to be of great significance for the island. The apostle Paul, a Roman citizen, was a prisoner on a ship sailing for Rome. The ship ran into a fierce storm and capsized. Paul was washed ashore on the coast of Malta. He stayed on the island for three months, during which time he set up Malta's first Christian community. This story is related in the Bible (Acts 27). The bay where St Paul was cast ashore still carries his name.

▲ *Remains of Roman rule can be seen in many places on Malta. This well-preserved Roman villa is in the old capital Rabat.*

▼ *St Paul's Bay, where the apostle Paul was washed ashore in* AD 59.

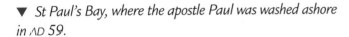

▲ *The streets and buildings of Mdina show a number of different styles, including Italianate and Arabic.*

Arab rule

The Roman occupation lasted until around AD 400, when the Roman Empire collapsed. For the next four centuries, Malta was part of the Byzantine (Eastern) Empire. In AD 870, Arabs captured the island. They reduced the size of the capital city, Melita, and built walls around it to defend it against attack. The section of the city within the walls was called Mdina ('fortified city') and the part without was known as Rabat ('the suburbs'). The names are still used today, although they now form two separate cities very close together. The architecture in both cities shows the Arabic influence, and this is also evident in the Maltese language, which uses many Arabic words.

The Arabs controlled the island for more than 200 years, after which it fell to the Normans. In the following centuries the island was ruled by various European powers, including the Spanish in 1282. The Maltese suffered greatly under Spanish rule. They were exploited and endured repeated attacks at the hands of North African and Turkish pirates.

The Knights of St John

The history of Malta took a very different turn in 1530, when Emperor Charles V handed the island over to the military order of the Knights of St John of Jerusalem (see page 42), who had been living on the island of Rhodes, but had been driven from their home by the Muslim Turks. The knights brought many changes to Malta. They moved the capital to a newly built settlement on the coast, Valletta, which was much easier to defend than a city in the middle of the island.

When the Holy Roman Emperor Charles V handed Malta over to the Knights of the Order of St John, he asked for something in return. Every year, the knights had to give him the gift of a falcon. The birds were kept in the Buskett Gardens in Valletta.

▶ *The Knights of St John, or the Hospitaller Knights, was an order of monastic knights formed to tend the sick during the twelfth-century Crusades. In the sixteenth century they built a large hospital, the Sacra Infermeria, on Malta. These models are from an exhibition in Valletta that explains the knights' history on Malta.*

In 1565 the Turks tried to seize Malta from the Knights of St John. Despite being greatly outnumbered, the knights withstood a siege of four months, after which the Turkish threat slowly diminished. Not only was the island itself successfully defended, but a halt was also put to the increasing influence of Islam from Africa, securing Christianity on the islands. The knights spent the next two centuries establishing their own society and culture on Malta. They built churches, palaces and a hospital in Valletta. Watchtowers on the coast enabled the knights to watch out for potential attackers coming from across the sea.

British occupation

In 1798, the French emperor Napoleon put an end to the knights' rule on Malta. He attacked the island and drove them off without even giving them a chance to gather their possessions. Everything was seized by Napoleon, including many religious treasures. But the French occupation only lasted for two years. The Maltese called on the British for help, with whose support the French were driven from the island in 1800.

After the success of the campaign, the Maltese invited the British to remain there, and Malta fell under British rule. As the island was strategically placed for British naval bases and trading posts, it was officially made a British Crown Colony in 1814.

Right from the start, however, the Maltese began campaigning for more political freedom. They realised that the trade links established by the British weren't doing them much good, and by the beginning of the twentieth century there was a great deal of social unrest. In 1921 Malta gained limited independence and was given its own parliament, but this was revoked 15 years later. During the Second World War (1939–45), the presence of a British naval fleet based at Malta prompted attacks from both the Italian and German Air Forces. Many houses were destroyed; thousands of people were killed and many of the survivors suffered severe hardship. For their courage and determination during this terrible time, the people of Malta were awarded the George Cross – the highest civilian award for bravery – in 1942. The country achieved full independence in 1964 and became a republic in 1974.

▲ *The British influence can still be seen on the islands; this street sign is written in Maltese and English.*

▶ *This plaque commemorates Malta becoming an independent republic in 1974.*

The Country

Malta comprises a small archipelago in the middle of the Mediterranean Sea. It consists of the islands Malta, Gozo and Comino, and the smaller, unpopulated islands of Cominetto and Filfla. It lies some 100 km off the southern coast of Sicily, and 290 km east of the North African coast.

There are around 397,000 people living on the Maltese islands. Ninety per cent of the population inhabits the largest island, Malta. Around 28,000 people live on Gozo, while Comino is barely inhabited, with only a small farming community.

The islands are very small. Malta measures 27 km from north to south at its longest point, and about 15 km from east to west. Gozo is much smaller – less than one third of the size of Malta – and Comino is only three square kilometres in size. Malta is one of the world's most densely populated islands, with 1,398 inhabitants per square kilometre.

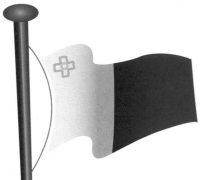

▲ *The Maltese national flag has two stripes – white and red. The cross on the white block is the George Cross, awarded to the people of Malta during the Second World War.*

▼ *The tiny island of Comino, with its rocky coastline and almost deserted coves, has very few inhabitants and is now a protected nature reserve because of the flora and fauna that flourish there.*

Malta

The Maltese landscape is mostly low and flat, with a few hills and many cliffs along the coastline. There are no mountains, lakes or rivers on the island, and its general appearance is bare and rocky. The coastline is rocky too; there are a few sandy beaches but most of them are pebble or shingle. Malta's predominant colour is ochre, a pale-brownish yellow – this is due to the limestone rocks that dominate the island. Many of the houses are built of this local limestone. Because the island has such a high population density there is very little vegetation. The towns and villages around the capital, Valletta, and the nearby city of Sliema have spread so much that they have converged.

The most fertile land lies in the south and east of the island. Small fields are divided by stone walls to prevent the fertile soil being washed away during heavy rainfall. This farming technique was introduced to Malta by the Arabs. The Dingli Cliffs, on the south coast, are around 200 metres high and sweep down to the sea in terraces (see page 5). Their clay soil is very fertile.

▲ Stone walls protect the fields, preventing soil from being washed away.

◄ There are ferries that run between the three main Maltese islands, as well as between certain points on Malta itself. This ticket is for the ferry that runs between Valletta and Sliema and other points along the Marsamxett Harbour (see map on page 4).

◀ A boat leaves Malta for Gozo every half-hour. The journey takes just over 20 minutes.

Gozo

Gozo lies only about 8 km off the tip of Malta, but it is very different from the main island. It is much greener than Malta and far less densely populated. The landscape is characterised by flat-topped hills and steep valleys. The towns are less sprawling and most of them are made up of groups of houses clustered round parish churches. The capital of Gozo is Victoria (also known as Rabat, the same name as one of the cities on the main island), which has a population of around 6,000.

The island's topsoil is clay, which retains water and makes the soil very rich. Much of the island is used for raising crops and livestock. Gozo is the archipelago's main food producer; products include grain, wine, milk and cheese. To the north lies Ramla Bay, one of the few places with a sandy beach, and therefore a popular tourist spot. Most of Gozo's beaches are relatively untouched by development, though, and the whole island is bursting with flora and fauna.

▼ Terraces are built on the hills across Gozo to stop the rich clay topsoil from washing downhill when it rains. Most of the islands' food products come from Gozo.

▲ *Travelling by boat from Malta to Gozo, you pass Comino. The building in the middle here is a watchtower, constructed by the Knights of St John.*

A legend surrounds Birbuba, a small village in the west of Gozo. It tells the story of a boy who was captured by pirates and taken away to be a slave. His sad mother went to the chapel where the alter bore a painting of St Dimitri. She begged the saint to bring her son back. Sometime later the boy returned. According to legend, Dimitri rose from the painting, followed the pirates, released the boy from captivity and returned him, unharmed, to his mother.

Comino

Comino's name comes from the Italian word for cumin, because the spice was cultivated on the island in the Middle Ages. Comino is a very dry, bare, rocky island, with just a few farms and a hotel. Not many people live there all year round. There were times when it was completely uninhabited and pirates used it as a hideaway. The watchtower on the coast dates from the time of the Knights of St John, when a handful of farmers and fishermen lived on Comino after the pirates had been driven away and it had been made safe for settlement.

On the western coast of the island is a stretch of water known as the Blue Lagoon. This is another popular tourist destination, because the clear water here is ideal for swimming and snorkelling. Ferries regularly run to this spot from the other islands.

Every weekend a priest visits from Gozo to celebrate mass in the island's tiny white church. There is also a small police station housing two police officers. Part of their job involves helping the meteorological office, for example, by measuring rainfall.

Climate

Malta has a Mediterranean climate, with long, hot summers lasting from April to October. The average summer temperature is 26°C. Winter – from November to March – is mild, with an average temperature of 12°C. Even in November, though, daytime temperatures can reach up to 25°C. Most of the rainfall occurs between the end of September and the end of April, often falling as short, heavy showers. Rainfall averages 500 mm a year. In summer, the sirocco, a strong, hot wind from the south or south-east, can raise temperatures to as high as 40°C and the heat can be oppressive.

Towns and cities

The capital of the main island is Valletta, which was built as a fortress town by the Knights of St John. It was named after an eminent member of the knights' order, Jean Parisot de la Valette. The city stands on the top of a hill on the peninsula that divides the Grand Harbour and the Marsamxett Harbour.

▲ *A street map of Valletta.*

Valletta

Valletta is one of the smallest capital cities in Europe, with a population of around 7,000. It is only 2 km from end to end. The city is laid out in a grid; the map above shows Valletta's straight roads and linear arrangement.

Because Malta occupies such a strategic position, and the Grand Harbour next to Valletta offered docks that could be

▲ *Valletta is built on a rocky hill, and there are many steep steps to climb when exploring the city.*

▶ *St John's Co-Cathedral in Valletta.*

'We've just been to see the Malta Experience,' says John, enthusiastically. 'That's a slide-show with music and commentary about the history of Malta,' he explains. 'We've come with the whole class, from St Augustino's College.'

The boys all wear their school uniforms, a tradition that remains from when the island was under British rule.

John's friend Peter isn't quite so impressed by the exhibition. 'I'd thought it would be more spectacular,' he laughs. 'But you definitely learn a lot,' he adds.

easily protected, the city has been used by several foreign nations over the centuries. In the early nineteenth century the British used it as the base for their Mediterranean fleet, and during the Second World War Valletta was the regional headquarters for the Allied countries. This resulted in it being targeted for bombing attacks during the war, and large parts of the city were destroyed.

However, several old buildings survived and there are many sites of historical interest in Valletta, as well as several museums and exhibitions dedicated to the history of the city and the Knights of St John in particular. The most important church is St John's Co-Cathedral, dedicated to St John the Baptist, patron saint of the Knights of St John. It was built between 1573 and 1578, although much of the decoration inside the church was added later and is very flamboyant and decorative. Napoleon and his army stole many of the church's treasures in 1798 (see page 9).

▲ The streets of Valletta are very narrow and it is difficult for traffic to squeeze through. There is a pedestrian area where people can walk around and shop freely out of the way of cars.

◀ The fronts of many houses in Valletta are adorned with enclosed wooden balconies. In times past the inhabitants would stand here and watch the activity in the streets below.

Sliema

Sliema has grown and spread out so much that it is not clear now exactly where Sliema ends and the capital Valletta begins. The city lies to the east of Marsamxett Harbour in the north-east of the island of Malta.

Sliema has more inhabitants than the capital – around 12,500. It is a bustling city and one of the most popular tourist destinations on the island because of its proximity to Valletta. There are many high-rise buildings and hotels here, as well as some of Malta's finest restaurants and cafés. Before the middle of the nineteenth century, though, Sliema and its nearby suburb St Julian's were mostly open fields with a few small villages where fishermen lived. It was only when the British arrived on Malta and began building summer homes in this area that Sliema started to grow. The Maltese middle classes soon followed suit and also began building houses here. After the Second World War even more people moved to Sliema from the surrounding towns, which were becoming overcrowded, and it became Malta's first proper tourist resort.

One of the city's finest features is the promenade, which runs along the waterfront. In the early evening locals and tourists alike come out to take a stroll here or to visit one of the many cafés along the promenade.

▲ *An old British mansion in Sliema. During the colonial period, wealthy British people lived in stately houses like this one along the waterfront in Sliema. Many of these have now been knocked down to make way for hotels and office blocks.*

▼ *Most of the shoreline in Sliema has flat, pebbly beaches. Steps lead down from the street to the waterfront at regular intervals along the promenade.*

▶ *St Paul's Cathedral in Mdina is one of the most popular visiting places for tourists. It was built in 1702 to replace an earlier cathedral that was destroyed by an earthquake.*

Rabat and Mdina

Rabat and Mdina lie in the middle of Malta. In Roman times they were both inside the same city walls and were called Melita, but the Arabs separated the two towns, thinking it would make them easier to defend, and they took two separate names.

In the middle of Rabat is St Paul's Church, named after the apostle Paul, who arrived on the island after a shipwreck and converted the people to Christianity. Legend has it that St Paul was imprisoned in a cave beneath where the church now stands. This is now known as St Paul's Grotto, and he is believed to have preached sermons there during his imprisonment. The church that stands on the site today was built in the seventeenth century on the orders of the Knights of St John.

Like Rabat, Mdina is a popular tourist destination. The city is not densely populated, and it has many winding streets that are too narrow for cars; because of this it has become known as the Silent City. Tourists come here to enjoy the peace and tranquility, but often there are so many of them that Mdina is anything but quiet! In the middle of the town stands St Paul's Cathedral – one of the most famous buildings on the island. Next to it is the Bishop's Palace, where the Archbishop of Malta lives.

Miriam stands in a narrow street. She is dressed in Mdina's traditional costume. 'I work for the Mdina Experience,' she says. 'I'm handing out leaflets about the show. It's all about the history of our town, the time of the Arabs, the Normans and, of course, the famous Maltese Knights.'

She has hung the plastic bags, which are full of leaflets about the show, on the iron bars of a window. 'There's a similar show in Valletta,' she tells us. 'But that one is about the history of the whole island.'

Which show is better? 'Why, ours of course!' she laughs, handing another leaflet to a passing tourist.

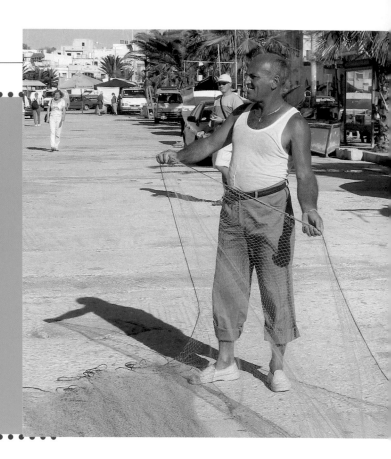

'Fishing is a wonderful way of life,' says Giorgo. He's checking the nets on the quayside. Giorgo heads out to sea every morning while it is still dark, to fish. He only stays a few hours. His wife waits for him to return and they sort the fish together; the catch is mostly dorados and lampukis. Then his wife sets off to sell the fish to the restaurants that line the harbour. These offer a wide variety of fish dishes all year round.

'There used to be a lot more fish in the sea,' says Giorgo. 'Now, there are only about 2,500 fishermen left in Malta. Many fish are now bred in fish farms. Who needs fishermen when you've got those?'

Marsaxlokk

Marsaxlokk (pronounced Marsashlok), on the eastern coast of Malta, is built on the side of a low hill. It sits in a picturesque bay, with lots of brightly painted fishing boats in the harbour. In the other direction, towards the sea, the view is not quite so idyllic. A power station has been built on a peninsula on the other side of the harbour, and further up the coast is the container port of Birzebugga.

▼ *The power station sits across the bay from Marsaxlokk.*

Many fishing-boats are painted with an eye, a tradition going back some 3,000 years, when the Phoenicians arrived on Malta. They decorated their boats with the eye of Horus, an Egyptian god, believing that it had protective powers and could keep them safe from harm.

▲ *The eye of Horus can be seen on many fishing boats in Malta. Fishermen believe it will protect them against dangers such as storms at sea.*

▼ *The medieval citadel and fortress on a hill in Victoria, built by the Knights of St John.*

Victoria

Victoria is the capital of Gozo. It is named after Queen Victoria, but the people who live there tend to use its older name, Rabat. In the centre of Victoria, on a hill, stands the medieval citadel and fortress, where the Knights of St John lived in the seventeenth century. The entrance leads to a small square with a church. On the left are the law courts and, to the right is the episcopal palace. The citadel is so large and self-contained that it is a town in its own right.

Gozo is greener and more rural than Malta. It is also less densely populated, with plenty of room for farmland. The island is so small that it can easily be explored by bicycle.

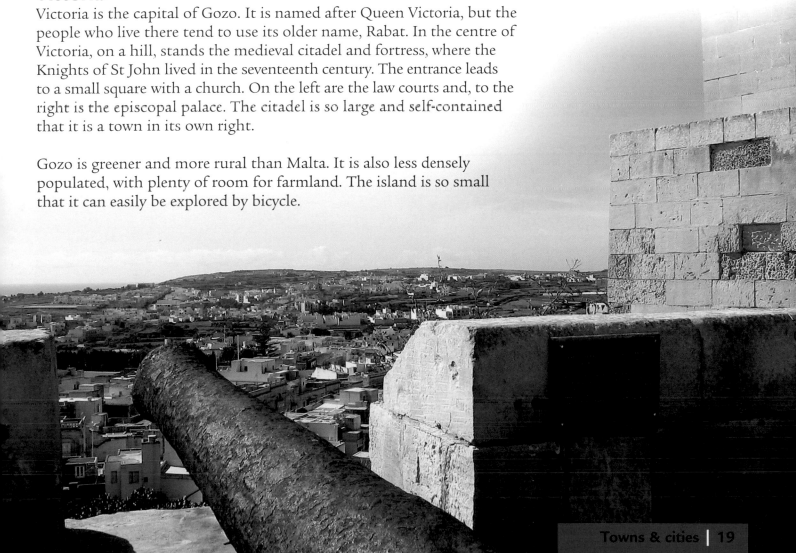

People and culture

In 1536, the Maltese knight Jean Quintin d'Autun estimated the number of people living on the Maltese islands to be 20,000. The population has grown dramatically since then, and today Malta is the most densely populated country in Europe, with around 397,000 inhabitants.

▼ *This table shows the growth of the population on the island of Malta since the sixteenth century.*

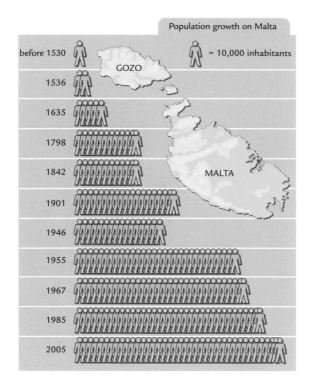

Population growth on Malta

👤 = 10,000 inhabitants

before 1530	
1536	
1635	
1798	
1842	
1901	
1946	
1955	
1967	
1985	
2005	

GOZO

MALTA

Although there are more people per square kilometre than anywhere else in Europe, more Maltese live outside Malta than on the island itself. Since the beginning of the twentieth century, young men especially have sought their fortunes elsewhere, driven out by unemployment on the islands. After the Second World War, many Maltese emigrated to Australia, the USA and Canada. It is estimated that some two million Maltese currently live abroad.

Many different peoples have occupied and settled on Malta throughout its history, and today there is still a mixture of nationalities and cultures to be found across the island. There are people of British, Italian and Arabic origin, as well as people from other countries, such as Spain and Sicily. Street signs are often shown in both Maltese and English, and some places even use the Italian names given them by the Knights of St John in the sixteenth century.

Family ties

Maltese families are very close and look after each others' welfare. As a result there are very few homeless people or beggars on the streets. Neither are there city slums. The grandmother, nanna, plays an important role in family life, looking after the children when the parents are working or shopping, and often cooking for the whole family. There are not many old-people's homes on Malta; most elderly people live with their children.

▶ *Members of Maltese families are usually very close to one another, and enjoy spending time together.*

Language

Maltese is a Semitic language, closely linked to Arabic and Hebrew, and strongly influenced by English and Italian. For a long time Maltese was only a spoken language; it was first written down at the beginning of the twentieth century. The Maltese alphabet has 29 letters: five vowels and 24 consonants. It uses Latin script.

Since Malta's independence in 1964, Maltese has been the national language. Up to about 30 years before this, Italian was Malta's second language, but now English is the other official language on the island, and almost all Maltese people speak English fluently.

Maltese words

Good morning	bongu
Thank you	grazzi
There you are	jek joghgbok
Beach	ramla
Yes	iva
No	le
Near to	ta'
Harbour	marsa
Goodbye	sahha

1	wiehed
2	tnejn
3	tlieta
4	erbgha
5	hamsa
6	sitta
7	sebegha
8	tmienja
9	disgha
10	ghaxzra

◀ Locals and tourists enjoy a drink outside a café in Sliema on a warm summer day.

▼ 'Merhba' means 'welcome' in Maltese and comes from the Turkish word 'Merhaba', which means 'hello'.

▲ *The neo-Gothic church of Our Lady of Lourdes stands high above the small town of Mgarr on the island of Gozo. Churches like this and the one in Nadur (see box), were often built on hilltops overlooking the towns.*

Nadur, a village on Gozo, lies in the middle of fertile farmland. The priest and the villagers could not agree on a place to build the village church. The feud went on for a long time, until one of the farmers decided he'd had enough and filled his cart with the heavy bricks that were intended for the church. He harnessed his donkey to the cart and encouraged it along, praying as he went. Suddenly, at the highest point on the island, the donkey stopped; the location for the church had been found.

Religion

Malta has around 300 churches and they are all well attended. More than 90 per cent of the population is Roman Catholic. Malta is an independent archdiocese, which means it has its own archbishop, who lives in the Bishop's Palace next to St Paul's Cathedral in Mdina.

In the summer months, many villages and towns hold *festas* to celebrate their own patron saint's days. These occasions are colourful events, with processions and bands. Everyone puts on their best clothes and the villages try to outdo one another with lavish celebrations. There are often fireworks in the evening.

Religion is an important part of life on the Maltese islands. Many bus drivers keep a devotional picture on the dashboard, or a statue of the Virgin Mary, decorated with fairy lights.

▶ *A procession celebrating the local patron saint in a village on Gozo.*

Media

The national broadcasting corporation on Malta is called the Public Broadcasting Services. There are three television channels, one public channel and two privatised commercial stations. There is also a cable network giving access to 49 television channels, around 15 of which are Italian. There are 11 radio stations in addition to local radio. Local radio stations are only allowed to broadcast within a range of 2.5 km.

Government

Malta has been a republic, with a president as head of state, since 1974. The president is chosen by parliament (the House of Representatives) for a five-year term of office. Since 1987 the parliament has had 65 members, all chosen by a constituency voting system. There are 13 constituencies. The president appoints the member of parliament who has the most support from inside the parliament as prime minister. The prime minister then appoints the other ministers and secretaries of state, who must all be members of parliament. A separate minister represents the interests of Gozo. Malta is a member of the British Commonwealth.

There are no counties on Malta; the country is divided into parishes. Since 1966 two political parties have been represented in parliament: the Maltese Labour Party and the Christian Democratic Party, *Partit Nazzjonalista* (PN). Each political party receives the endorsement of a national newspaper.

▼ *The Grand Master's Palace in Valletta has been Malta's seat of government since it was built in the 1570s. In its time it has housed the Grand Masters and the British governors, during colonial rule. Now it is home to the parliament and the president's office.*

Education

On Malta, all children from the ages of five to 16 have to attend school. The education system is similar to the one in the UK, and was established during the period of British rule on the island. Education is free and is given in Maltese and English. Primary schools are co-educational, but boys and girls are taught separately at secondary level.

For the first six years, children attend primary school. When they are 11 they move on to secondary education at schools called Junior Lyceums or Secondary Orientation/Guidance. The first two years of secondary education are called 'orientation years'. During this time pupils study several subjects to decide what they would like to do in the next level of secondary school. They are also given guidance about what they might like to do when they leave school.

Upper secondary school

Between the ages of 13 and 16, Maltese children attend upper secondary school. At the end of this time they take exams in order to receive their diplomas – the Secondary Education Certificate. Once they have this, students are no longer under any obligation to stay in full-time education and are free to start work if they want to. If they wish to continue their education, however, they can study for a further two years at the Sixth-Form Upper Lyceum. The diploma they receive if they successfully pass their exams there means they can go on to university.

University

There is one university on Malta, which was established in 1592. Students can study a range of subjects, including economics, architecture, engineering and medicine. The university has a good reputation and people come from overseas to study here. Teaching at the University of Malta is in English.

If students want vocational training, they can attend the technical college or the school for tourism on Malta.

◀ *A teacher helps children with wooden puzzles at a primary school. Children start school at the age of five on Malta.*

All schoolchildren on Malta wear a uniform. As well as the state schools, there are Roman Catholic schools. The boys at this school wear a blue uniform. The girls' uniform is pink. They are pupils at a private school in Zebbug. Many schools organise excursions to historical sites, where children can learn about their country's long and volatile history. The secondary-school children make notes that they will write up as a report when they get back to school.

▲ *These children are looking around Mdina and its old buildings and churches. Many field trips are organised to historical sites across Malta.*

▼ *A school trip to the temple complex of Hagar Qim (see page 7).*

Cuisine

Maltese cuisine shows the influence of the many cultures that have settled on the island over the centuries, as well as the influence of its neighbouring countries, in particular Sicily. Typical British food like fish and chips can also be found on Malta.

Like many Mediterranean countries, Malta has an abundance of fish, and fish and seafood dishes are available in most restaurants. One popular fish caught locally is lampuki, which is similar

▲▼ *Maltese specialities in this restaurant include rabbit with spaghetti, lampuki in caper sauce, fresh tuna and stewed octopus.*

to mackerel, with firm white flesh. Swordfish and tuna are also common. One particular speciality is a fish soup called aljotta; this can be made with different types of fish, and is cooked with potatoes and garlic. Despite the availability of fresh fish, about two thirds of the fish consumed on the island are imported.

Fruit and vegetables

The island cannot grow enough fruit and vegetables to provide for all the people who live there, so most of these products are imported. One of the most popular vegetable dishes on Malta is minestrone, or vegetable soup. Soup made of qarabali – baby marrows (similar to courgettes) – is also a favourite Maltese dish, as is pastry – a delicacy called pastizzi (ricotta cheese and egg wrapped in thin crisp pastry) is available all over the island.

Meat

Like many other food products, much meat is imported. However, there are several traditional Maltese recipes and a variety of exotic food is available on the island. There are plenty of rabbits on Malta, and a typical local dish is braised rabbit cooked with wine and lots of garlic. Stewed and stuffed meats are also popular.

▲ *Meats like rabbit or beef are stewed or braised with vegetables and often cooked with wine.*

◄ *The Maltese tend to prefer sweet pastries, gateaux, fruit salad or ice cream to baked, hot desserts.*

Recipe for vermicelli omelette

Ingredients
400g vermicelli or spaghetti
3 eggs
2 dessertspoonfuls Parmesan cheese
Oil
Salt
Freshly milled pepper
Chopped parsley

Boil the vermicelli for five minutes in a saucepan of salted water and then drain it. Beat the eggs and add the Parmesan cheese and parsley. Mix the egg mixture with the vermicelli. Add salt and pepper. Put some oil in a frying-pan and slide the mixture into the pan. Fry until lightly browned, then turn the omelette over. Garnish with parsley and serve.

▲ *Vermicelli omelette is made with pasta and cheese.*

▼ *Diet Kinnie was introduced in 1984.*

Kinnie

After the Second World War, several different types of cola appeared on the market. A Maltese company came up with its own variety, using unpeeled, bitter oranges as the basic ingredient, and adding 18 different herbs and mineral water. The result was Kinnie, a unique soft drink that is only available on Malta. It is very popular with the locals.

Transport

Malta has 1,742 km of roads, most of which are paved. The main road runs from north to south and is road No. 1. Although this is mostly dual carriageway, it does not class as a motorway.

▼ *Road signs indicating directions are white on a blue background.*

The roads are extremely busy and suffer quite a lot of wear and tear. However, efforts are being made to improve the condition of many roads on Malta. The maximum speed limit in the villages and towns is 40 kilometres per hour. Outside the built-up areas it is 65 kilometres per hour.

The Maltese drive on the left, a custom left over from the time of British rule. Another custom is that road and street signs are often given in English as well as Maltese, which can help tourists find their way around more easily. Many of the streets in the towns and cities are made more for pedestrians than cars, as they are quite narrow. For this reason, many Maltese prefer to travel around using public transport.

▼ *Some roads in Malta are being closed in preparation for resurfacing to improve their condition.*

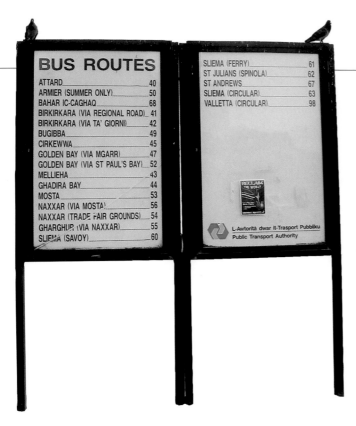

BUS ROUTES

ATTARD_____40
ARMIER (SUMMER ONLY)_____50
BAHAR IC-CAGHAQ_____68
BIRKIRKARA (VIA REGIONAL ROAD)_41
BIRKIRKARA (VIA TA' GIORNI)____42
BUGIBBA_____49
CIRKEWWA_____45
GOLDEN BAY (VIA MGARR)_____47
GOLDEN BAY (VIA ST PAUL'S BAY)_52
MELLIEHA_____43
GHADIRA BAY_____44
MOSTA_____53
NAXXAR (VIA MOSTA)_____56
NAXXAR (TRADE FAIR GROUNDS)___54
GHARGHUR (VIA NAXXAR)_____55
SLIEMA (SAVOY)_____60

SLIEMA (FERRY)_____61
ST JULIANS (SPINOLA)_____62
ST ANDREWS_____67
SLIEMA (CIRCULAR)_____63
VALLETTA (CIRCULAR)_____98

L-Awtorità dwar it-Trasport Pubbliku
Public Transport Authority

◄ *Boards indicating which bus goes to which part of the island make it easy for visitors to travel around.*

Public transport

The best way to travel around Malta is by bus, and they are the most efficient form of public transport (there are no railway lines on the island). From Central Square in Valletta buses go in all directions to most parts of the island.

Some of the buses date back to the 1950s, when Malta was still under British rule; however, there are now many newer buses running as well. The doors on the buses are always open – it never really gets cold on Malta – and in the summer this helps a cool breeze pass through the vehicle, as it can get quite stuffy.

The other form of public transport on Malta is the ferry. Ferries run between the three islands on a regular basis, as well as doing shuttle runs across the bays and harbours.

▼ *Buses, even the older ones, are convenient and inexpensive on Malta.*

▶ *The old harbour in Valletta.*

Shipping

Malta is well placed for the shipping industry. Situated right in the middle of the Mediterranean, it lies close to many major shipping lanes. Shipping has always been one of the islands' most important activities. Valletta's old harbour is still operational, and a new container port has been built at Birzebugga. The containers are unloaded quickly and the ships don't have to remain in the harbour for long.

Aviation

Malta has its own airline, Air Malta, which operates direct flights to many destinations, including England, the Netherlands, Germany, Italy, Greece, Norway, Spain, Switzerland, Bulgaria, Cyprus, Morocco, Tunisia and Egypt. The airline uses modern aircraft, such as the Boeing 737 and the Airbus.

There is only one airport, situated near Luqa in the south-east. Most of the aircraft that take off from here are operated by Air Malta.

▲ *The new container port at Birzebugga.*

▼ *Malta's international airport is near Luqa.*

▼ *Air Malta is the national airline.*

The economy

Much of Malta's economy is dependent on foreign trade. Its most important trading partners are the USA, Germany, France, the UK and Italy.

Many of the ships that sail under the Maltese flag are not actually of Maltese origin, but belong to German, Italian or Greek shipping companies. These companies choose to register their ships in Malta – for example in Valletta – because the tax duties they have to pay are lower than they would be in their own countries. Whether this will remain the case now that Malta is part of the European Union remains to be seen.

Malta enjoys a good relationship with these countries, and with the others with which it trades. International relations will be assisted further by membership of the EU, particularly in import and export to other EU countries.

▲ A container storage area at the port of Birzebugga.

▼ Wind-powered water-pumps dot the landscape across Malta. Water lies deep under the ground in some places.

Import and export

Malta provides just 20 per cent of its own food requirements; the rest is imported. Farms are small. Only six per cent of the workforce is employed in the agricultural sector and some of the employees regard this as a supplementary income.

The most important imports are equipment for transport and machinery, semi-manufactured products such as petroleum, and foodstuffs. Its key import partners are Italy (19 per cent), France (14 per cent), the UK (8 per cent) and Germany (7 per cent).

Agricultural produce such as flowers, plants and potatoes are exported, along with cauliflowers, grapes, wheat and barley. Other exports include clothing, textiles, glass and pottery. Key export partners are Singapore (17 per cent), the USA (12 per cent), the UK (9 per cent) and Germany (9 per cent). Goods exported to the UK include machinery and transport equipment, and clothing.

▼ *Lace made on Gozo is renowned for its beauty and is exported to many countries.*

▲ *This is a potato field on Gozo. Potatoes are one of Malta's most important exports.*

Maltas

Most potatoes in Europe are harvested in September and October. In the old days, people used to buy bags of potatoes in bulk, storing them in their cellars so they would have a constant supply throughout the winter. However, this affected the quality of the potatoes, and by the end of the season they had gone soft.

Suddenly, potatoes started appearing in the shops in April. They came from Malta, where the climate was so mild that potatoes could survive the winter. They were given the nickname 'Maltas' as early as the nineteenth century, but they are actually grown on Gozo. Ninety per cent of the total harvest goes to the Netherlands. The German and Danish markets consume the rest.

Industry

An enormous shipyard remains on Malta from the British-colonial period, and ship-building and repair are still two of the most important industries on the island. The old shipyard was taken over by the government after the islands gained independence, and it is now privately owned.

Some 2,700 people work at the Malta Dry Docks at Valletta. It can accommodate ships weighing up to 300,000 tonnes. Steel plates are manufactured at various engineering works on the site and it can even repair damaged screws (propellor-blades).

▶ *Some of Malta's key exports are electronic and electrical equipment and parts.*

▼ *For many years, the British naval dockyards were an important part of the Maltese economy. Even though they have now been privatised, they are still a flourishing industrial centre.*

▶ *The Playmobile factory, producing its famous toys, is situated in Zejtun and employs around 700 people. The toys are shipped to countries all over Europe.*

Tourism

Tourism is Malta's most important industry and its main source of income. Tourists fall into two main categories: young people who come to the island in the summer, and older people who generally come in spring and autumn.

The younger tourists spend most of their days on the beach and their nights in the bars and night-clubs in the cities. Watersports such as diving and surfing are popular pastimes for younger tourists and locals.

▲ *The weather remains fine enough to sunbathe on the beaches until late autumn on Malta.*

◄ *A small seaside restaurant at Ramla Bay.*

▼ *Ramla Bay on Gozo is one of the few sandy beaches on the islands. It is almost 500 metres long. The dune area behind the bay is unique to Gozo.*

Nearly everywhere in Malta caters for tourists. In the cities there are already many hotels, and more are being built all the time. Restaurants enjoy a roaring trade and open-air cafés along the seafront are very popular, as tourists can taste local delicacies while listening to the waves crash against the rocks on the beaches.

Guided tours

Spring and autumn see the influx of mainly older tourists, who regard their stay on Malta as a mid-season break. Most of them come to see something of the island, and usually take guided tours to the many historical sites at places like Valletta, Mdina and Gozo. The most popular guided tours are those to the churches and cathedrals, the museums and the ancient temple complexes.

Jimmy and his friend are walking along the beach. Every now and then they wade into the sea and scoop up large piles of seaweed with a net and throw it on to the beach. They then rake through the seaweed with their hands, looking carefully. 'We're trying to find a particular type of worm that lives in the seaweed,' Jimmy explains. He and his friend enjoy fishing as a hobby, and they put these worms on their fish-hooks to use as bait. 'The flatfish love them!' Jimmy tells us. Anglers can often been seen searching through piles of seaweed on Malta's beaches.

▼ *Seaside hotels dot the rocky coastline all around Malta.*

◄ *Tourists exploring the narrow streets and old buildings of Valletta.*

Working in the tourist industry

A large part of the Maltese workforce is employed in the tourism sector. Around 1,500 students leave school to take up employment in tourism each year, with a qualification to work in the industry. Cooks, waiters and tour-guides all train here. Over one million tourists visit Malta every year, the majority of whom come from the UK.

The British feel at home on Malta because many British traditions are followed and English is spoken. Malta is also popular with German and Scandinavian tourists. Many schools and training-colleges give short English-language courses.

Tourists can rent cars on Malta, but many of them are put off by the busy traffic. Most tourists decide to travel by bus. The bus network covers virtually the entire island.

◄ *One lira is worth about 1.5 British pounds, or 2.3 euros.*

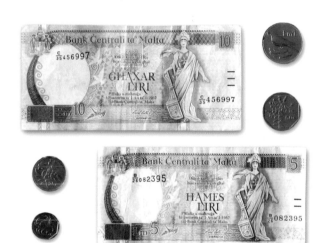

Currency

When Malta joined the European Union it accepted the obligation to switch its currency to the euro. However, this is unlikely to become the islands' official currency until 2008. Until then, the currency remains the Maltese lira (also known as pounds). There are coins in denominations of 1 lira, 50, 25, 10, 5, 2 and 1 cents, and banknotes to the value of 2, 5, 10 and 20 liri.

► *The Archeological Museum in Valletta.*

▲ A sign welcomes tourists to Popeye Village.

▼ Over the course of seven months, the movie village of Sweethaven was built on Malta for the film Popeye – a village of brightly painted wooden houses.

Filming on Malta

Many film directors consider Malta an ideal location for filming because of the stunning scenery. It has a magnificent rocky coastline boasting lots of creeks and bays, and the weather is nearly always sunny.

More than 80 films have been made on Malta in the past 50 years. The most famous in recent years is *Troy*, which filmed on Malta for 10 weeks in 2003; the set for the city of Troy was built at Fort Ricasoli. Other movies partly filmed on Malta include *Gladiator* and *The League of Extraordinary Gentlemen*.

One of the most popular tourist attractions on the island is Popeye Village, a film set built for the musical movie *Popeye*, based on the cartoon hero. The film set is still there. Visitors can walk round the village, go inside Popeye's home, the fire station, post office, the shop and the school.

Nature

The Maltese islands are too small for large animals to live in the wild there. However, there are plenty of small mammals such as rabbits, weasels and bats. There are also several types of lizard. A breed of dog known as the Maltese lion, once depicted on ancient vases, can still be found on Malta.

Apart from the blue rock thrush, there are not many unusual birds on the island. Sparrows, larks, jackdaws, blackbirds and finches are the most common. In spring and autumn, migratory birds stop on the islands. The inhabitants used to shoot birds for sport – the birds would arrive on the island exhausted, which made them easy prey. People turned a blind eye to this sport for a long time, but now it is strictly forbidden.

Birdlife Malta is a nature conservation organisation focusing on birds. There are also a few nature reserves to protect animals and plants.

▲ *The blue rock thrush is the national bird of Malta and is strictly protected by law. The birds usually make their nests in the cliffs of the coastal regions.*

▼ *Wild dogs can sometimes be seen on Malta. The scrub vegetation provides a habitat for mammals such as ferrets and weasels.*

Marine life

The sea along the coast supports a variety of marine life, such as swordfish, stingrays, sea bream, squid and octopuses. The shallow coastal inlets make an ideal breeding ground for young fish. The water is warm and there is plenty of food.

Trees

Trees are scarce on Malta. In ancient times the islands were covered with forests, but the trees were all cut down to provide timber for houses and boats, and to use as firewood. Buskett Gardens – the hunting-grounds of the Verdala Palace near Rabat, established by the Knights – is the only place where small groups of trees still grow from centuries ago. Here you can find lemon and olive trees, palm trees, pine and spruce.

▲ *Inlets like the Blue Lagoon offer the perfect conditions for marine life to breed.*

All the trees that grow in other Mediterranean countries, such as the almond, fig, carob and olive tree, can be found elsewhere on the island, but there are very few of each variety.

▼ *The sea thistle grows on a small area of dunes on Gozo.*

Plants

Despite the lack of trees, several varieties of plants and shrubs flourish in the warm climate of the Maltese islands. Cacti can be found in many places, thriving in the hot conditions. There are also a thorny species of shrub, the maquis, and aromatic herbs such as thyme, basil and oregano. The national plant is the Maltese centaury, which grows on the cliff-tops.

◀ *Agave thrives in the dry heat of Malta (see box).*

▼ *Oleanders and lantanas have been planted along some of the roads.*

There are hundreds of varieties of agave. After about 15 years the plant produces flowers, which grow on an enormous stalk that shoots out of the ground. This costs the plant so much energy that it usually dies after it has bloomed.

▼ *The presence of reeds in this part of the island indicates that there is groundwater.*

The Knights of St Joh

The Knights of St John were a religious military order, originally founded to tend the sick and wounded crusader knights. The Knights of St John played an important part in Malta's history, but their story begins long before they came to the island in the sixteenth century.

The Crusades

By the eleventh century the Byzantine Empire extended from south-east Europe to the western part of the Middle East. The capital was Constantinople (now Istanbul). In around 1071 the Turks conquered large parts of the Byzantine Empire and Palestine. When this news reached the pope he called upon the Christian nations to go to Palestine to fight against the Turks. It was a scandal, he said, that the 'ungodly' Turks – as he called the Muslims – should have captured the Holy Land. He wanted the country to be returned to Christendom, and promised those who helped that their sins would be forgiven and that they would not have to pay taxes when they returned. Many people, including some adventurous knights, responded to the pope's call, and in 1096 the Crusades were launched.

The Maltese Cross

The Maltese Cross (see opposite) is the symbol used both by Malta and by the Knights of St John. It was originally used by Italian merchants from Amalfi, who established Jerusalem's first hospital in around 1050. The cross represented the republic of Amalfi – the state of Italy didn't exist then. The four arms of the cross symbolise the virtues strength, justice, moderation and perseverance. The eight points represent the eight *langues* (languages or tongues, see page 44).

◄ *The Mdina Festival is held every year. During this cultural festival people wear historical costumes, celebrating and reliving Malta's ancient past related to the Knights of St John. Here, they stand in front of the cathedral in Mdina.*

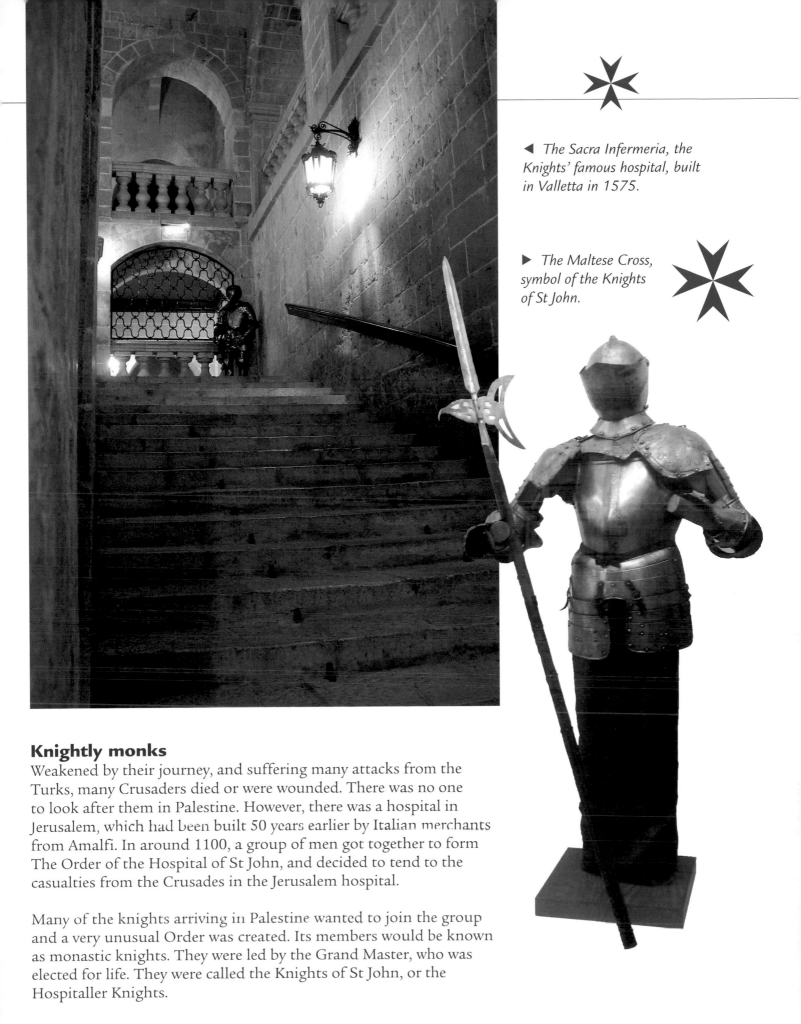

◀ *The Sacra Infermeria, the Knights' famous hospital, built in Valletta in 1575.*

▶ *The Maltese Cross, symbol of the Knights of St John.*

Knightly monks

Weakened by their journey, and suffering many attacks from the Turks, many Crusaders died or were wounded. There was no one to look after them in Palestine. However, there was a hospital in Jerusalem, which had been built 50 years earlier by Italian merchants from Amalfi. In around 1100, a group of men got together to form The Order of the Hospital of St John, and decided to tend to the casualties from the Crusades in the Jerusalem hospital.

Many of the knights arriving in Palestine wanted to join the group and a very unusual Order was created. Its members would be known as monastic knights. They were led by the Grand Master, who was elected for life. They were called the Knights of St John, or the Hospitaller Knights.

Langues

Besides their battle duties on board the galleys, the knights' main priority was to look after the sick. Even the Grand Master had to work one day a week in the hospital. The knights all came from different countries and spoke different languages. A group of knights who spoke the same language was called a *Langue*. There were eight different *Langues*, which included knights from France, Provence, the Auvergne, Italy, Germany, Castile and Portugal. Only members of the aristocracy could join the Order.

In 1291 the Turks drove the knights out of Palestine; they fled to the Mediterranean island of Cyprus, but didn't stay there long. In 1310 they captured the island of Rhodes and decided to settle there.

Rhodes

The Turks advanced further and further into Europe, capturing Greece and the Asian part of what is now Turkey. The conquest of the Byzantine capital Constantinople in 1453 marked the end of the Byzantine Empire. The Knights of St John, meanwhile, were continuing to attack Turkish ships, which angered the Turks. Sultan Suleiman II arrived on Rhodes with a huge army. After much resistance the knights finally surrendered. They were sent off in boats and drifted around looking for a new base from which to engage the enemy.

In 1530, Holy Roman Emperor Charles V presented Malta to the knights. In exchange, the knights had to give the emperor a falcon every year (see page 8).

The knights were shocked when they first laid eyes on Malta, it was so dry and bare. They were expecting the Turks to catch up with them, so they built fortresses on the coast almost immediately.

▲ *Evidence of the knights' time on Malta can be seen all over the island.*

▼ *St Elmo's fort (on the left, at the far end of the peninsula) was built by the knights in 1552 as a defence against an imminent attack by the Turks.*

AUBERGE DE PROVENCE.

THIS BUILDING, ERECTED IN 1575, WAS OCCUPIED BY THE KNIGHTS OF ST JOHN FROM PROVENCE WHO WERE ENTRUSTED WITH THE DEFENCE OF ST JOHN'S CAVALIER AND ITS BASTION. THEIR CHIEF WAS THE GRAND COMMANDER OF THE ORDER.

▲ *The magnificent interior of St John's Co-Cathedral, with the tomb of one of the knights (left).*

In 1565 the Turks stormed Malta. The Maltese joined the knights against the enemy in a siege that lasted for over four months. In the end the Turkish army gave up and retreated.

After the Turkish siege, the knights decided to restructure Valletta as a fortified city in case of future attacks. This may have frightened off the Turks, since they never made any attempt to attack Malta and the Knights of St John again. There followed a period of increasing prosperity.

▲ *A terrace in Valletta. Behind it is the Maltese National Library, housing the archives of the Knights of St John from their inception in the twelfth century until they left Malta in 1798.*

The knights wanted to recreate the opulent way of life that most of them had enjoyed before they came to Malta. Cultural and artistic activities such as music, sculpture and painting flourished. Some of the islanders were employed by the knights as servants, profiting from the order's new-found prosperity. But many of them continued to toil in the fields, and remained poor. In fact, a widening gap appeared between the knights, who were becoming increasingly wealthy, and the local population, who remained impoverished.

In 1798 the French emperor Napoleon and his fleet arrived on the island. Many of the knights were French and unsure of where their allegiance should lie. They surrendered with little or no resistance.

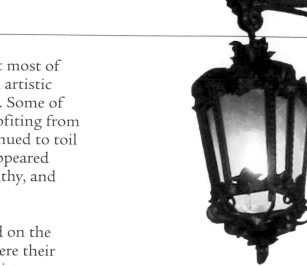

◀ *After the Turkish siege, the fortified town of Valletta was built by the knights in case the Turks returned to attack them again.*

The knights today

Now that the knights had been driven away from Malta – their home for many centuries – they did not know where to go next. At first they travelled to St Petersburg in Russia, where Tsar Paul I became their patron in 1799. However, they did not settle there for long. After moving around further they finally settled in Rome, where the Grand Master still holds residence.

▲ The prison that was once used by the knights is situated under the hospital that they originally built to tend the sick when they arrived in Malta.

Today, the Order of the Knights of St John is divided into two sections: the Protestant Order of St John and the Roman Catholic Order of Malta. The knights are involved in the provision of humanitarian aid. Beatrix, Queen of the Netherlands, is a knight of the Protestant branch of the Order of Malta.

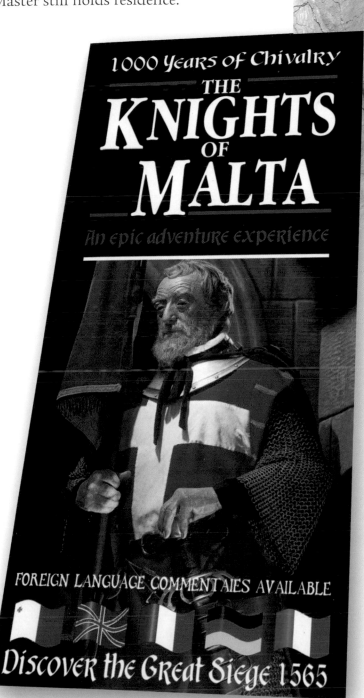

◄ The Maltese people are proud of the knights' association with their island, and commemorate their time there with several exhibitions. This leaflet advertises a historical re-enactment of the siege, in a museum in Valletta.

Glossary

Archipelago A group of islands.

Byzantine Empire The eastern part of the Roman Empire after it was divided in AD 395.

Crown Colony Land overseas from Britain that was under the jurisdiction of the British king or queen.

Crusades A series of military campaigns in which knights from Christian states tried to 'free' the Holy Land and other countries from Muslim occupation.

Islam The laws and beliefs of the Muslim religion.

Megalithic The era in which large stone monuments were erected for social or religious reasons, dating back as far as 5000 BC.

Middle Ages The period from around AD 500 to 1450.

Phoenicia An ancient country around the ninth to the sixth centuries BC, made up of city-states along the Mediterranean coast of present-day Lebanon.

Stone Age The earliest period in technological history, when tools and weapons were made from stone.

Index

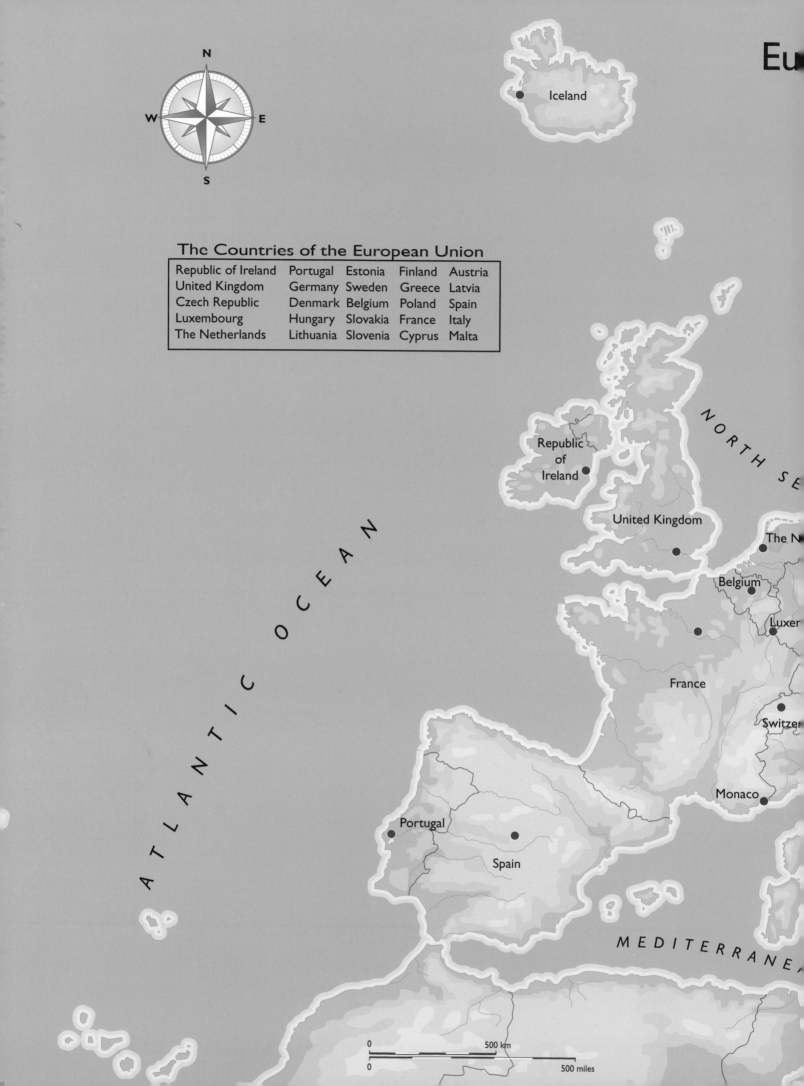

Eu

The Countries of the European Union

Republic of Ireland	Portugal	Estonia	Finland	Austria
United Kingdom	Germany	Sweden	Greece	Latvia
Czech Republic	Denmark	Belgium	Poland	Spain
Luxembourg	Hungary	Slovakia	France	Italy
The Netherlands	Lithuania	Slovenia	Cyprus	Malta

Iceland

NORTH SE

Republic of Ireland

United Kingdom

The N

Belgium

Luxer

France

Switzer

Monaco

Portugal

Spain

MEDITERRANEA

ATLANTIC OCEAN

N
W   E
S

0   500 km

0   500 miles